STRUM IT
GUITAR

AUTHENTIC CHORDS
ORIGINAL KEYS
COMPLETE SONGS

# the very best of TOM PETTY

MW00799683

**Cover photo by Dennis Callahan**

ISBN-13: 978-0-634-03161-8
ISBN-10: 0-634-03161-9

HAL•LEONARD®
CORPORATION
7777 W. BLUEMOUND RD. P.O. BOX 13819 MILWAUKEE, WI 53213

Visit Hal Leonard Online at
**www.halleonard.com**

# CONTENTS

5    STRUM IT GUITAR LEGEND

6    AMERICAN GIRL

12    BREAKDOWN

9    DON'T COME AROUND HERE NO MORE

14    DON'T DO ME LIKE THAT

17    EVEN THE LOSERS

20    A FACE IN THE CROWD

22    FREE FALLIN'

28    HERE COMES MY GIRL

30    I NEED TO KNOW

25    I WON'T BACK DOWN

32    INTO THE GREAT WIDE OPEN

34    LEARNING TO FLY

36    LISTEN TO HER HEART

38    REFUGEE

41    RUNNIN' DOWN A DREAM

44    STOP DRAGGIN' MY HEART AROUND

# STRUM IT GUITAR LEGEND

Strum It is the series designed especially to get you playing (and singing!) along with your favorite songs. The idea is simple – the songs are arranged using their original keys in lead sheet format, providing you with the authentic chords for each song, beginning to end. Rhythm slashes are written above the staff. Strum the chords in the rhythm indicated. Use the chord diagrams found at the top of the first page of the arrangement for the appropriate chord voicings. The melody and lyrics are also shown to help you keep your spot and sing along.

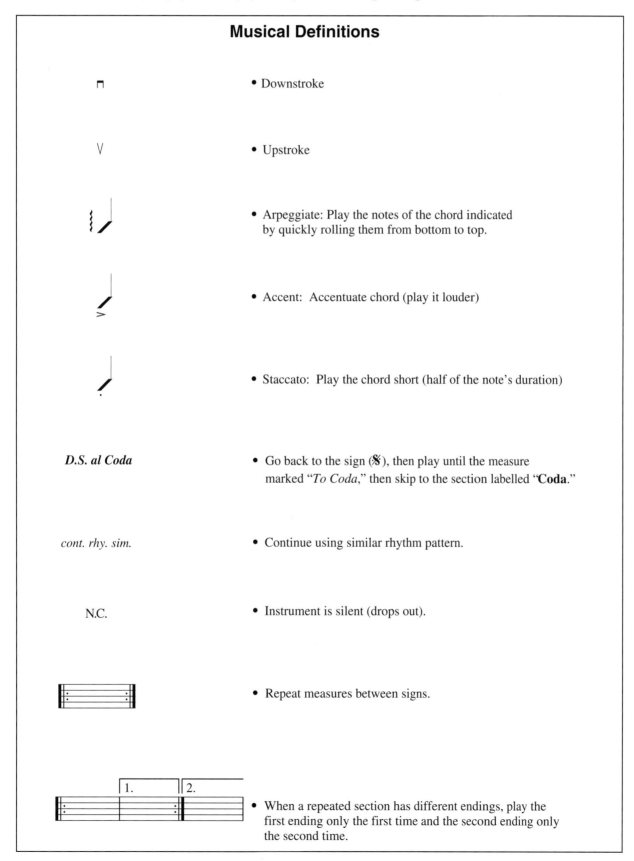

## Musical Definitions

| | |
|---|---|
| ⊓ | • Downstroke |
| V | • Upstroke |
| | • Arpeggiate: Play the notes of the chord indicated by quickly rolling them from bottom to top. |
| | • Accent: Accentuate chord (play it louder) |
| | • Staccato: Play the chord short (half of the note's duration) |
| *D.S. al Coda* | • Go back to the sign (𝄋), then play until the measure marked "*To Coda*," then skip to the section labelled "**Coda**." |
| *cont. rhy. sim.* | • Continue using similar rhythm pattern. |
| N.C. | • Instrument is silent (drops out). |
| | • Repeat measures between signs. |
| 1.   2. | • When a repeated section has different endings, play the first ending only the first time and the second ending only the second time. |

# American Girl

**Words and Music by Tom Petty**

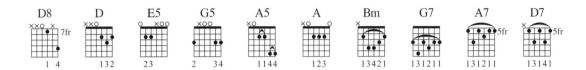

**Intro**
**Moderate Rock**

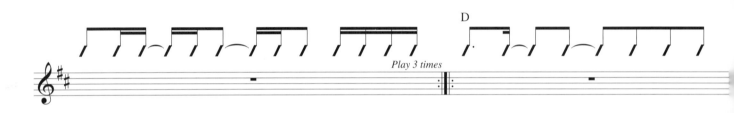

**Verse**

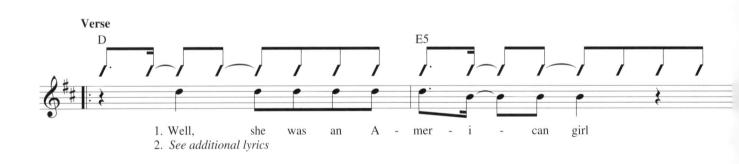

1. Well, she was an A - mer - i - can girl
2. *See additional lyrics*

raised on prom - is - es. ___   She could-n't help think - in' ___ that there was a

lit - tle more _ to life     some - where _ else. __     Af - ter all it was a

great big _ world _____     with lots of plac - es ___ to run to. __

Yeah, and if ___ she had to die     try - in', she _____     had one lit - tle prom - ise

**Chorus**

she was gon - na keep. _____     Oh yeah,     al - right.

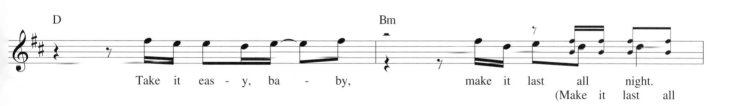

Take it eas - y, ba - by,     make it last all night.
(Make it last all

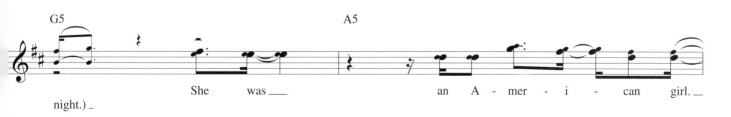

She was ___     an A - mer - i - can girl. __

night.) _

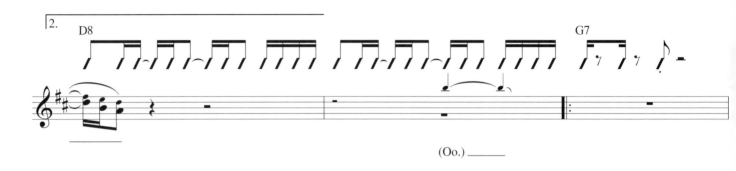

(Oo.) _____

*Repeat and fade*

**Outro-Guitar Solo**

*Additional Lyrics*

2. Well, it was kinda cold that night.
   She stood all alone over the balcony.
   Yeah, she could hear the cars roll by
   Out on four-forty-one
   Like waves crashin' on the beach.
   And for one desperate moment there,
   He crept back in her memory.
   God, it's so painful when
   Somethin' that is so close
   Is still so far out of reach.

# Don't Come Around Here No More

**Words and Music by Tom Petty and David Stewart**

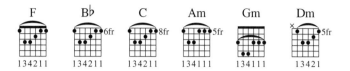

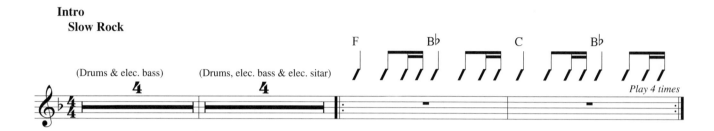

**Intro**
**Slow Rock**

(Drums & elec. bass)    (Drums, elec. bass & elec. sitar)

*Play 4 times*

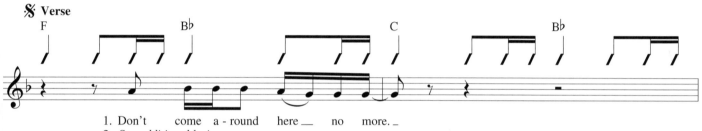

**Verse**

1. Don't come a-round here __ no more. __
2. *See additional lyrics*

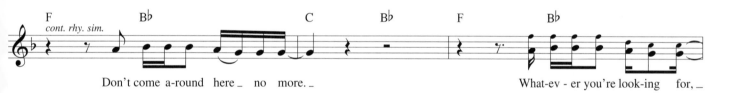

Don't come a-round here __ no more. __    What-ev-er you're look-ing for, __

___    don't come a-round here __ no more. __
(Hey!)

**Pre-Chorus**

I've giv-en up.    I've giv-en up.
(Giv-en up.    Stop!)    Giv-en up.    Stop!

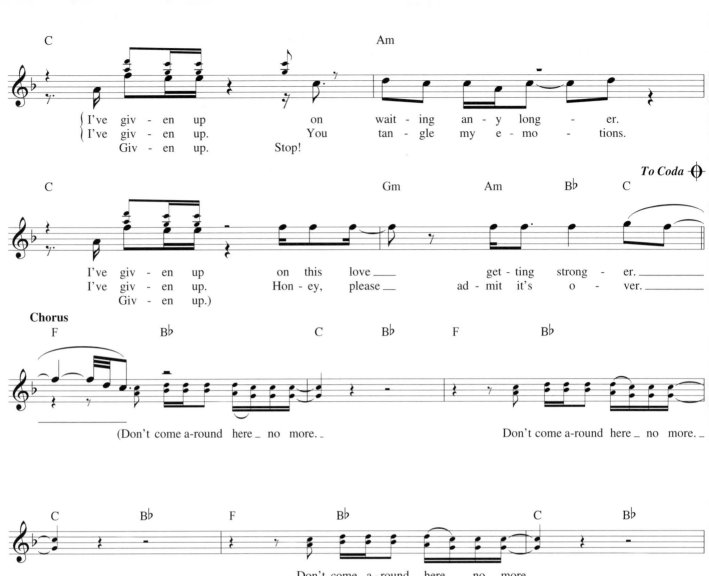

**Chorus**

(Don't come a-round here no more.)

Don't come a-round here no more.

Don't come a-round here no more.

*D.S. al Coda*

**Coda**
**Interlude**

Don't come a-round here no more.)

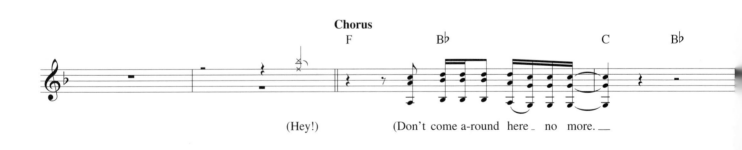

**Chorus**

(Hey!)

(Don't come a-round here no more.

Don't come a-round here no more.

Don't come a-round here no more.

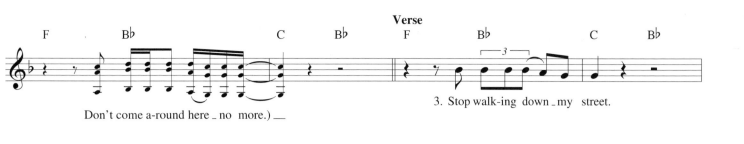

Don't come a-round here _ no more.) _

**Verse**

3. Stop walk-ing down _ my street.

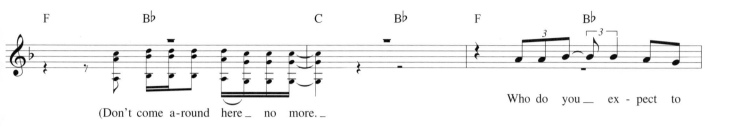

(Don't come a-round here _ no more. _

Who do you _ ex - pect to

meet? _____

Don't come a - round here _ no more.) _

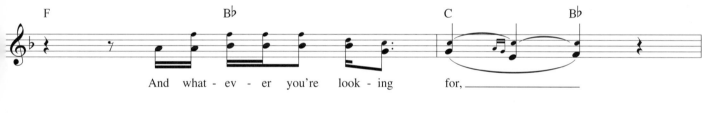

And what - ev - er you're look - ing for, _____

**Double-time feel**

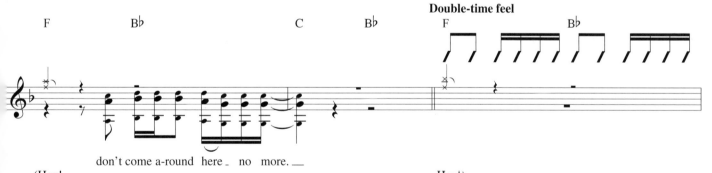

don't come a-round here _ no more. _

(Hey!                                                    Hey!)

**Outro**
w/ Voc. ad lib.                                          *Repeat and fade*

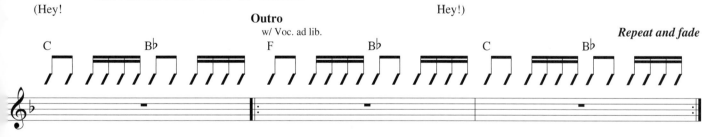

*Additional Lyrics*

2. Don't feel you anymore.
   You darken my door.
   Whatever you're looking for,
   (Hey!) Don't come around here no more.

# Breakdown

**Words and Music by Tom Petty**

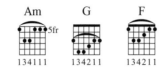

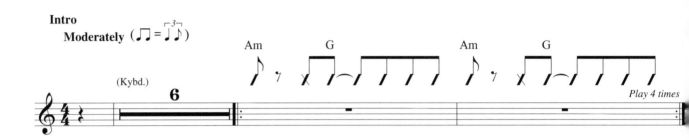

**Intro**
**Moderately**

(Kybd.)

Play 4 times

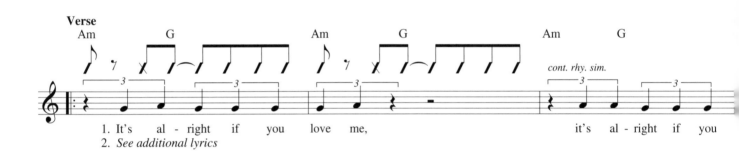

**Verse**

cont. rhy. sim.

1. It's al - right if you love me,         it's al - right if you
2. *See additional lyrics*

don't.         I'm not a - fraid of you run - nin' a - way, hon - ey,   I  get  the __ feel - ing you __

|1.
won't. __         *Whispered:* (I  said...)  say. _____            Ba - by.

|2.

**Chorus**

cont. rhy. sim.

Break - down,         go a - head,  give it to me.         Break - down,  hon - ey, take __

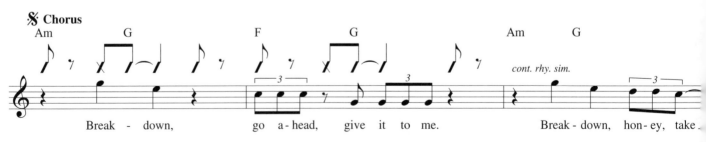

Additional Lyrics

2. There is no sense in pretending;
   Your eyes give you away.
   Somethin' inside you is feelin' like I do.
   We've said all there is to say.

# Don't Do Me Like That

**Words and Music by Tom Petty**

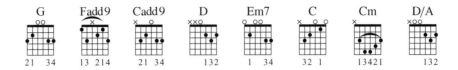

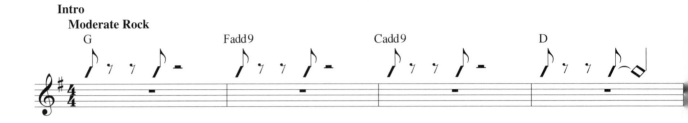

**Intro**
**Moderate Rock**

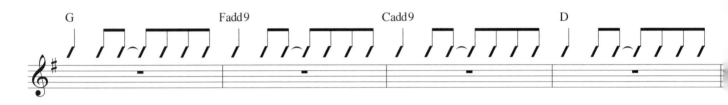

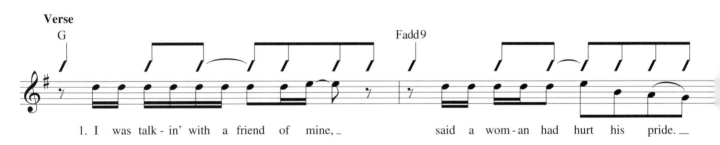

1. I was talk-in' with a friend of mine, ___ said a wom-an had hurt his pride. ___

Told him that she loved him so and turned a-round 'n' let him go.

Then he said, "You bet-ter watch your step or you're gon-na get hurt your-self. ___

**Chorus**

Some-one's gon-na tell you lies, cut you down to size." Don't do me like that,

don't do me like that.  What if I loved you, ba - by? _  Don't do me like that. _

Don't do me like that,  don't do me like that.  Some-day I might need you, ba - by.

**𝄋 Verse**

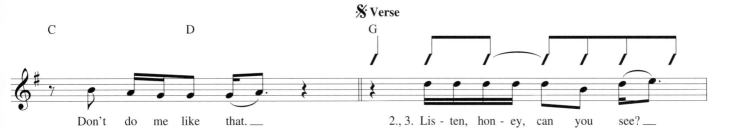

Don't do me like that. _  2., 3. Lis - ten, hon - ey, can you see? _

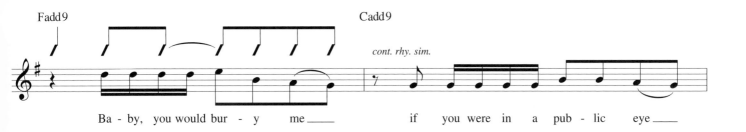

*cont. rhy. sim.*

Ba - by, you would bur - y me ___  if you were in a pub - lic eye ___

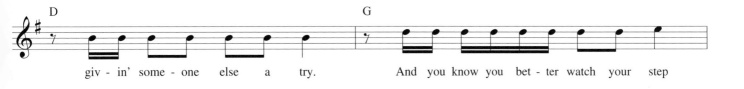

giv - in' some - one else a try.  And you know you bet - ter watch your step

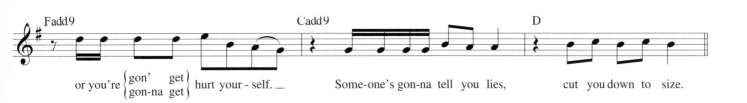

or you're {gon' get / gon-na get} hurt your - self. _  Some-one's gon-na tell you lies,  cut you down to size.

**Chorus**

Don't do me like that,  don't do me like that.  What if I loved you, ba - by? _

Don't, don't, don't, don't. Don't do me like that, don't do me like that.

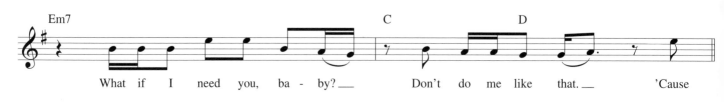

What if I need you, ba - by? ___ Don't do me like that. ___ 'Cause

**Bridge**

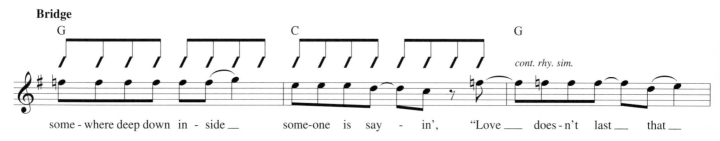

some - where deep down in - side ___ some-one is say - in', "Love ___ does-n't last ___ that ___

*D.S. al Coda*

long." ___ I've had this feel-in' in - side ___ night out and day ___ in, and

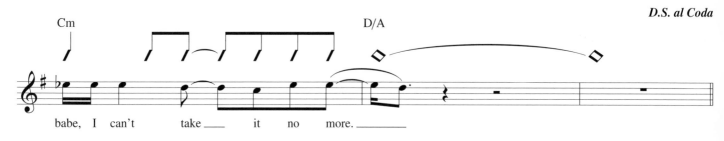

babe, I can't take ___ it no more. ___

⊕ **Coda**

I just ___ might need you, hon - ey. Don't do me like that. Now, wait.

**Outro**

Don't do me like that, don't do me like that.

*Repeat and fade*

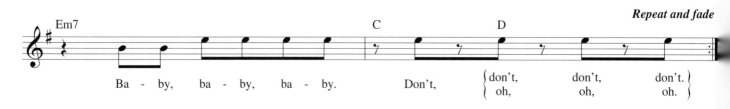

Ba - by, ba - by, ba - by. Don't, {don't, don't, don't.} {oh, oh, oh. }

16

# Even the Losers

**Words and Music by Tom Petty**

**Intro**
**Moderate Rock**

1. Well, it was mere-ly sum-mer, we sat___ on your__ roof.
2. *See additional lyrics*

**Verse**

*cont. rhy. sim.*

Yeah, _ we smoked cig-a-rettes and we stared _ at the moon. _____

And I showed _ you stars _ you nev-er could see.

Babe, it could-n't have been that eas-y to for-get a-bout me.

[1.]

[2.]

**% Chorus**

2. Ba-by, Ba-by, e-ven the los-ers,___

get luck-y some-times. _ E-ven the los - ers, _____

*To Coda* ⊕

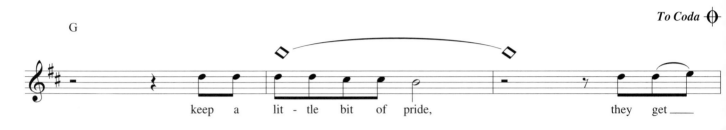

keep a lit-tle bit of pride, they get ____

**Guitar Solo**

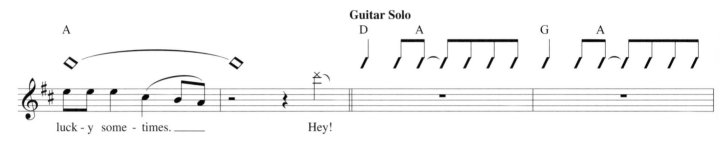

luck-y some-times. ____ Hey!

*cont. rhy. sim.*

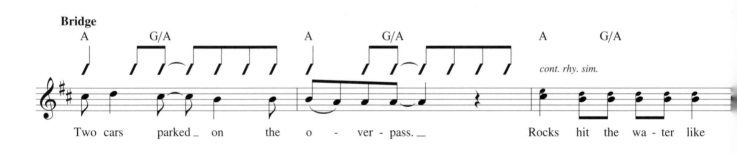

**Bridge**

Two cars parked _ on the o - ver - pass. _ Rocks hit the wa-ter like

bro - ken glass. ___ I should-'ve known _ right then it was too ___ good to last. _ God,

it's such a drag when you liv'n' in the past. __ Ba - by, e - ven the los -

**Coda**

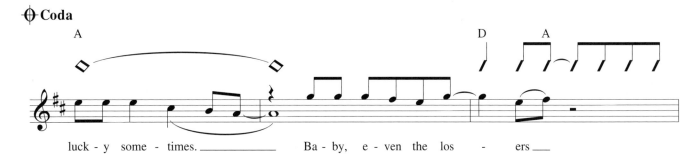

luck - y some - times. _____ Ba - by, e - ven the los - ers __

get luck - y some - times. _ E - ven the los -

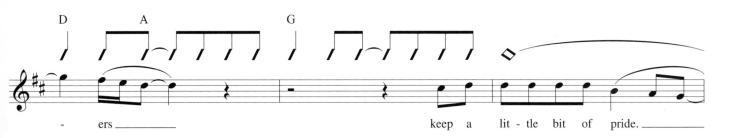

- ers _____ keep a lit - tle bit of pride. _____

__ Yeah, they get luck - y some - times. _____ Ba - by, e - ven the los -

**Outro**

- ers __ get luck - y some - times. _ E - ven the los -

*Additional Lyrics*

2. Baby, time meant nothin', anything seemed real.
   Yeah, you could kiss like fire and you made me feel,
   Like ev'ry word you said was meant to be.
   No, it couldn't have been that easy to forget about me.

# A Face in the Crowd

**Words and Music by Tom Petty and Jeff Lynne**

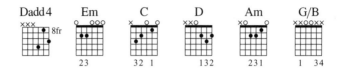

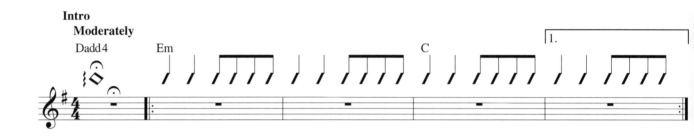

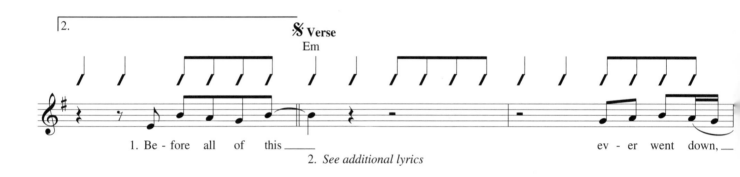

# Free Fallin'

## Words and Music by Tom Petty and Jeff Lynne

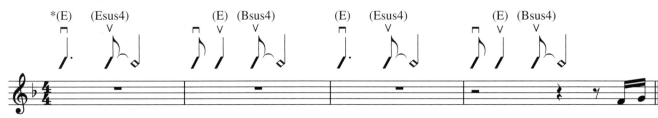

Capo I

**Intro**

**Moderately slow**

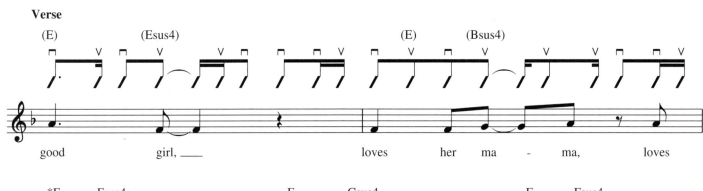

1. She's a

*Symbols in parentheses represent chord names respective to capoed guitar and do not reflect actual sounding chords.

**Verse**

good girl, ___ loves her ma - ma, loves

Je - sus ___ and A - mer - i - ca ___ too. ___ She's a good girl, ___

*Symbols in parentheses represent chord names respective to capoed guitar.
Symbols above reflect actual sounding chords.

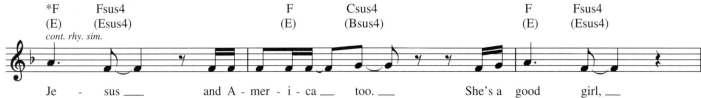

cra - zy 'bout ___ El - vis, loves hor - ses ___ and her boy-friend too. ___

**Verse**

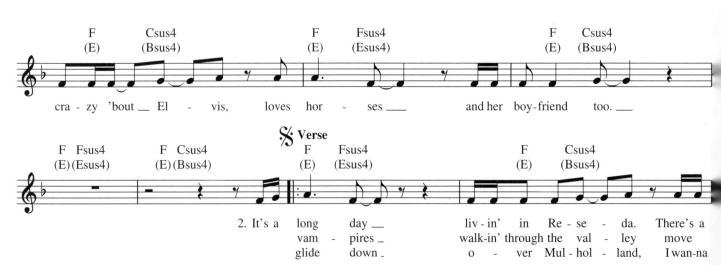

2. It's a long day ___ liv-in' in Re - se - da. There's a
vam - pires ___ walk-in' through the val - ley move
glide down ___ o - ver Mul - hol - land, I wan-na

free - way ___ run-nin' through the yard. ___ And I'm a bad boy ___ 'cause I
west down ___ Ven - tu - ra Boul-e-vard. ___ And all the bad boys ___ are
write her ___ name in the sky. ___ I'm gon-na free fall ___

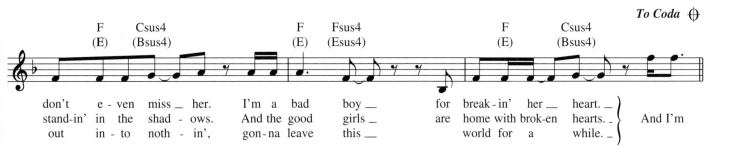

*To Coda*

don't e - ven miss ___ her. I'm a bad boy ___ for break - in' her ___ heart. ___
stand-in' in the shad - ows. And the good girls ___ are home with brok-en hearts. ___ } And I'm
out in - to noth - in', gon-na leave this ___ world for a while. ___

**Chorus**

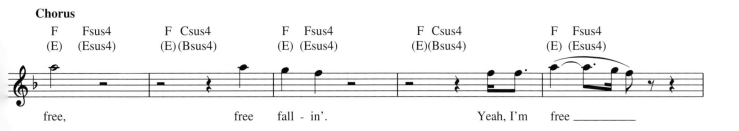

free, free fall - in'. Yeah, I'm free _____

**Interlude**

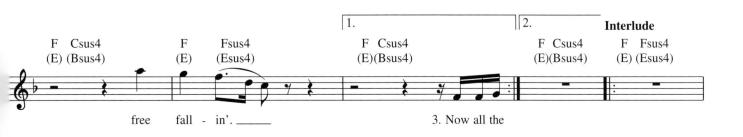

free fall - in'. _____ 3. Now all the

*D.S. al Coda*

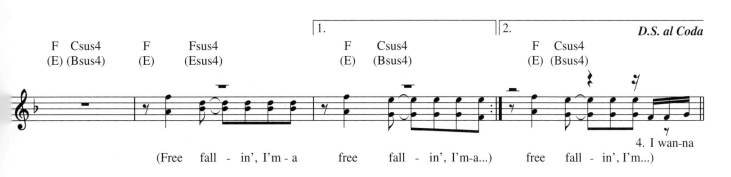

(Free fall - in', I'm - a free fall - in', I'm-a...) free fall - in', I'm...)

4. I wan-na

**23**

## ⊕ Coda

**Chorus**

free,
(fall - in', I'm - a  free  fall - in', I'm - a  free  fall - in', I'm - a

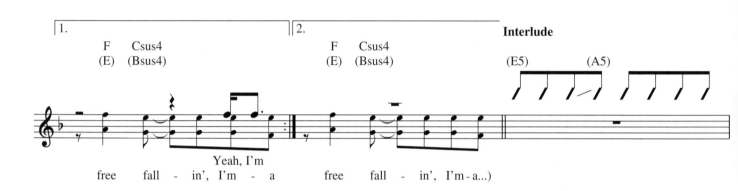

Yeah, I'm
free  fall - in', I'm - a  free  fall - in', I'm - a...)

**Interlude**

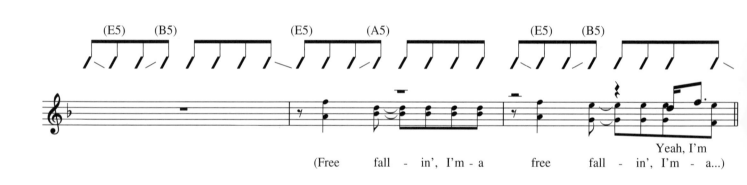

(Free  fall - in', I'm - a  free  fall - in', I'm - a...)

Yeah, I'm

**Outro-Chorus**

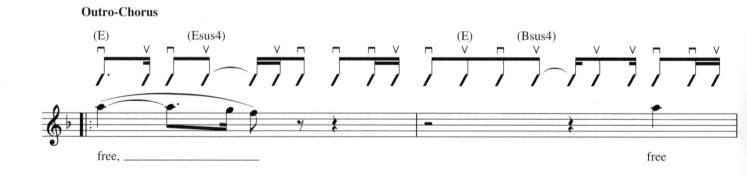

free, _____  free

*Repeat and fade*

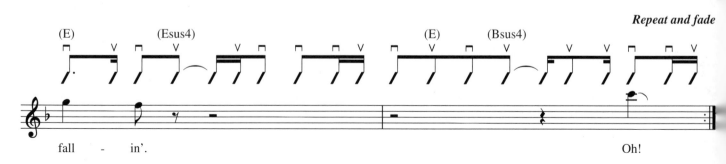

fall - in'.  Oh!

24

# I Won't Back Down

**Words and Music by Tom Petty and Jeff Lynne**

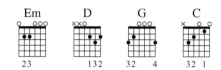

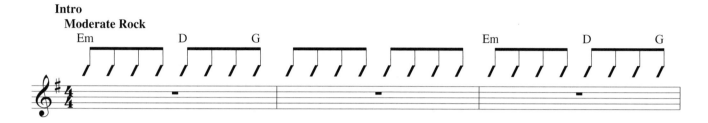

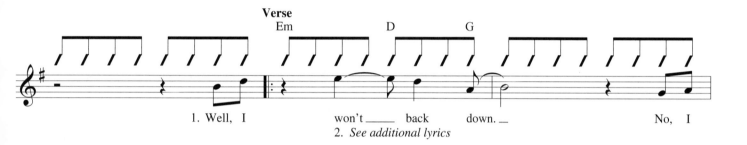

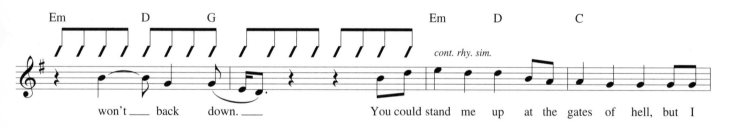

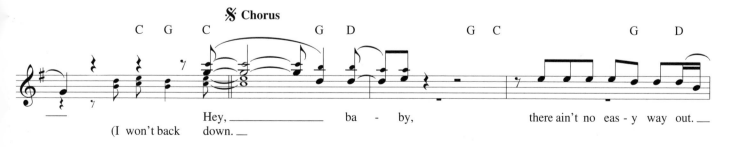

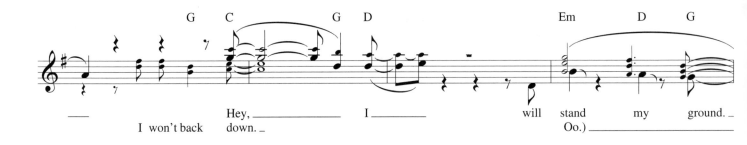

G    C        G  D            Em    D    G

Hey, _____ I _____ will stand my ground.
I won't back down. _

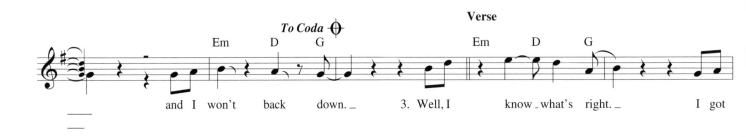

*To Coda* ⊕              **Verse**

Em    D    G         Em    D    G

and I won't back down. _    3. Well, I know _ what's right. _    I got

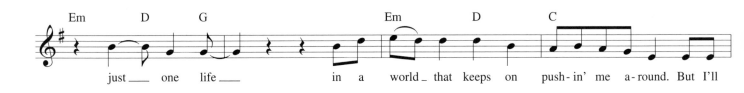

Em    D    G         Em    D    C

just _ one life _ in a world _ that keeps on push-in' me a-round. But I'll

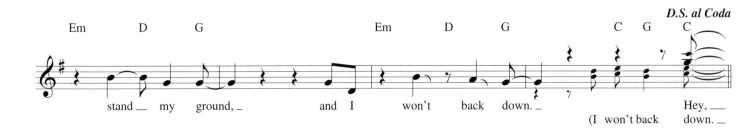

                                                *D.S. al Coda*

Em    D    G         Em    D    G    C  G  C

stand _ my ground, _ and I won't back down. _        Hey, _
(I won't back down. _

⊕ **Coda**

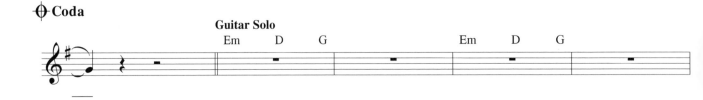

**Guitar Solo**

Em    D    G         Em    D    G

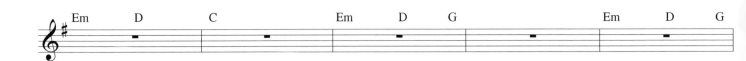

Em    D    C         Em    D    G         Em    D    G

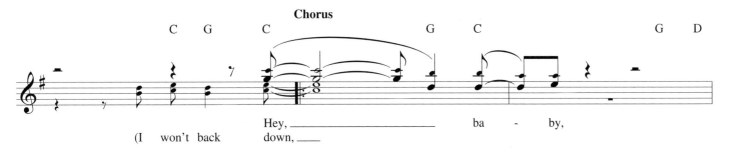

**Chorus**

Hey, _____ ba - by,
(I won't back down, \_\_\_\_\_

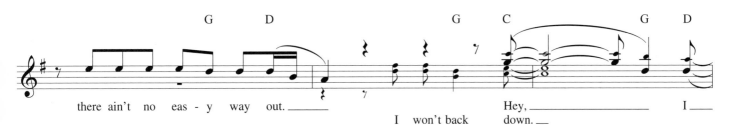

there ain't no eas - y way out. \_\_\_\_\_ Hey, _____ I \_\_\_
I won't back down. \_\_\_

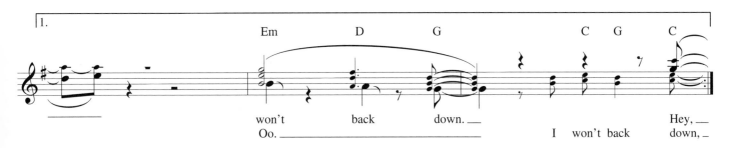

**1.**
_____ won't back down. \_\_\_ I won't back Hey, \_\_
Oo. _____ down, \_

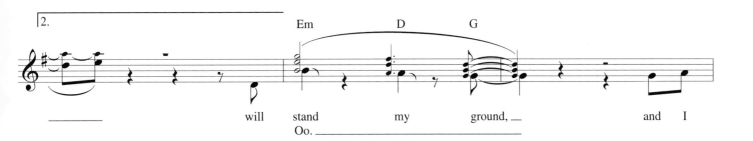

**2.**
_____ will stand my ground, \_\_ and I
Oo. _____

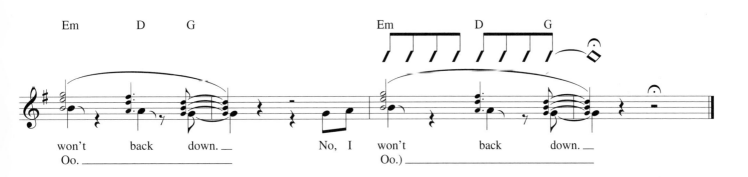

won't back down. \_\_ No, I won't back down. \_\_
Oo. _____ Oo.) _____

*Additional Lyrics*

2. No, I'll stand my ground.
   Won't be turned around.
   And I'll keep this world from draggin' me down,
   Gonna stand my ground.
   And I won't back down.

# Here Comes My Girl

**Words and Music by Tom Petty and Mike Campbell**

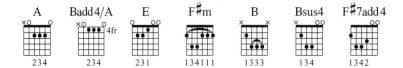

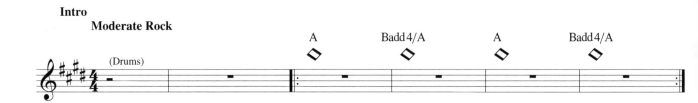

*Spoken:* 1. *You know sometimes I don't know why, but this old town just seems so hopeless.*
2., 3. *See additional lyrics*

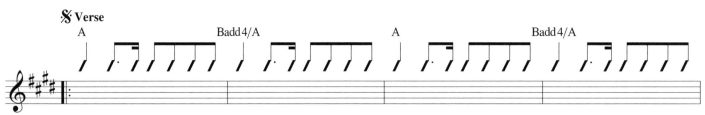

*I ain't really sure, but it seems I remember the good times were just a little bit more in focus.*

But when she puts __ her arms __ a - round __ me, __ I can some-how rise a-bove

it. Yeah, ol' man, when I got that lit-tle girl __ stand-in' right by my side, you know, I can

tell the whole _ wide _ world. Shout it, hey. Here comes my girl. _____

Here comes my girl. _____ Yeah, and she looks _

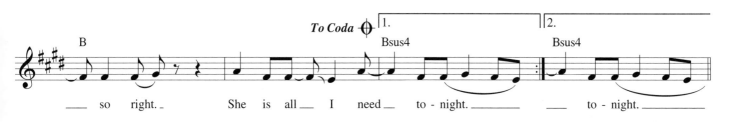

_ so right. _ She is all _ I need _ to - night. _____ _ to - night. _____

**Bridge**

*3rd time, D.S. al Coda*
*Play 3 times*

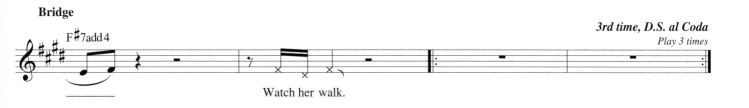

Watch her walk.

**Coda**

**Outro**

*Repeat and fade*

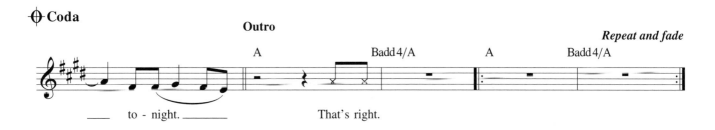

_ to - night. _____ That's right.

*Additional Lyrics*

2. Ev'ry now and then I get down to the end of the day,
   I have to stop, ask myself why I've done it.
   It just seems so useless to have to work so hard and
   Nothin' ever really seem to come from it.
   And then she looks me in the eye
   And says, "We're gonna last forever."
   Man, you know I can't begin to doubt it.
   Know that this feels so good and so free and so right.
   I know we ain't never gon' change our minds about it, hey.

3. Yeah, ev'ry time it seems like there ain't nothin' left no more
   I find myself havin' to reach out and grab hold of somethin'.
   Yeah, I just catch myself wonderin' and waitin' and worryin'
   About some silly little things that don't add up to nothin'.
   And then she looks me in the eye
   And says, "We're gonna last forever."
   Man, you know I can't begin to doubt it.
   Know that this feels so good and so free and so right.
   I know we ain't never gon' change our minds about it, hey.

# I Need to Know

**Words and Music by Tom Petty**

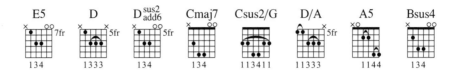

**Intro**
**Moderate Rock**

1. Well, the talk on the street says you might go so-lo.
2. *See additional lyrics*

Good friend of mine saw you leav-in' by your back door.

**% Chorus**

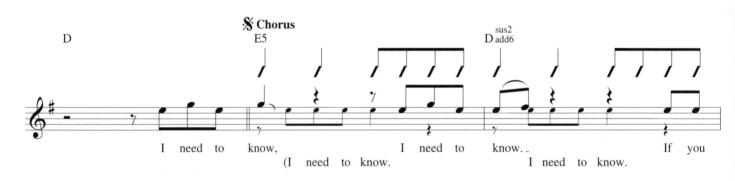

I need to know, I need to know. If you
(I need to know. I need to know.

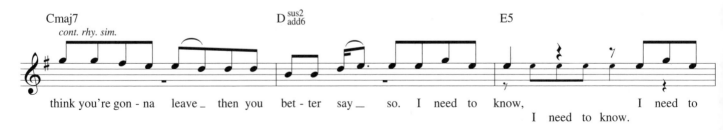

think you're gon-na leave then you bet-ter say so. I need to know, I need to
I need to know.

*Additional Lyrics*

2. Who would have thought that you'd fall for his line?
All of a sudden it's me on the outside.

# Into the Great Wide Open

**Words and Music by Tom Petty and Jeff Lynne**

*Additional Lyrics*

2. The papers said Ed always played from the heart.
He got an agent and a roadie named Bart.
They made a record and it went in the charts.
The sky was the limit.
His leather jacket had chains that would jingle.
They both met movie stars, partied and mingled.
Their A and R man said, "I don't hear a single."
The future was wide open.

# Learning to Fly

**Words and Music by Tom Petty and Jeff Lynne**

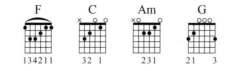

# Listen to Her Heart

**Words and Music by Tom Petty**

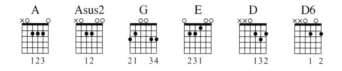

**Intro**
**Moderate Rock**

1. You think you're gon-na take her a-way, ___
2. *See additional lyrics*

with your mon-ey and your co - caine. You keep think-in' that her

mind is gon-na change, ___ but I know ev-'ry-thing is o - kay. She's gon-na

**Chorus**

lis-ten to her heart. ___ It's gon-na tell her what to

*Additional Lyrics*

2. You want me to think that I'm bein' used;
   You want her to think it's over.
   You can't see it doesn't matter what you do,
   An' buddy, you don't even know her.

# Refugee

**Words and Music by Tom Petty and Mike Campbell**

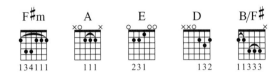

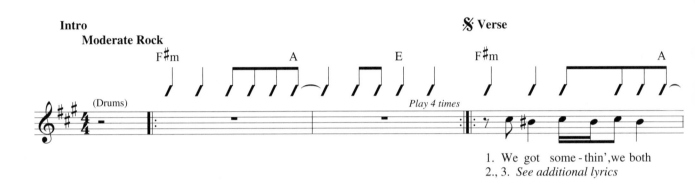

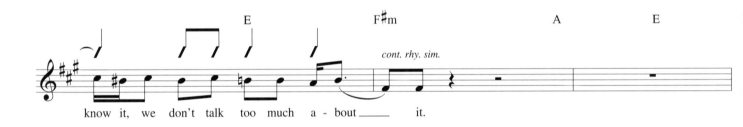

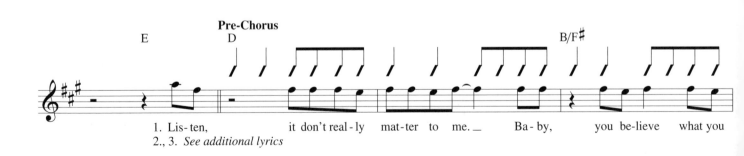

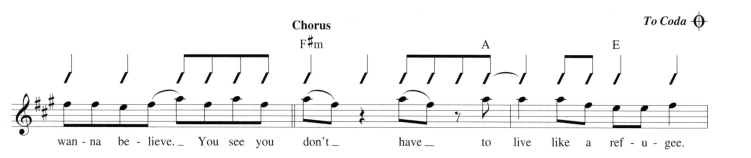

**Chorus**

wan - na be - lieve. _ You see you don't _ have _ to live like a ref - u - gee.

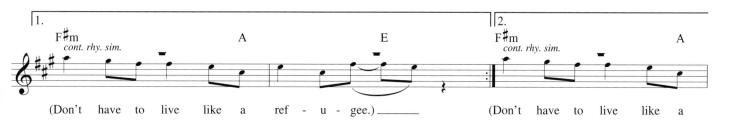

1. (Don't have to live like a ref - u - gee.) _____

2. (Don't have to live like a

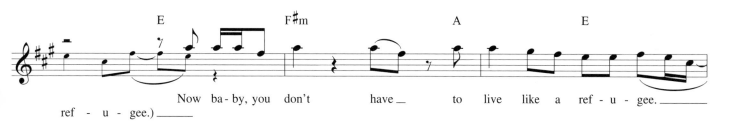

Now ba - by, you don't have _ to live like a ref - u - gee. _____

ref - u - gee.) _____

**Bridge**

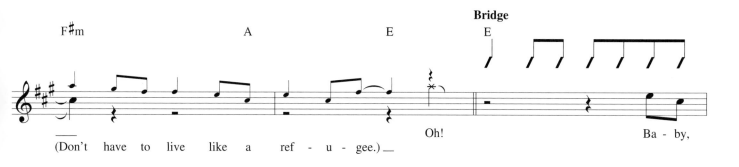

(Don't have to live like a ref - u - gee.) _    Oh!    Ba - by,

we ain't the first. _    I'm sure a lot of oth - er lov - ers been burned. _

Right _ now this seems _ real ____ to you, _ but it's one of those things you got to feel

**Organ/Guitar Solo**

*4th time, D.S. al Coda*

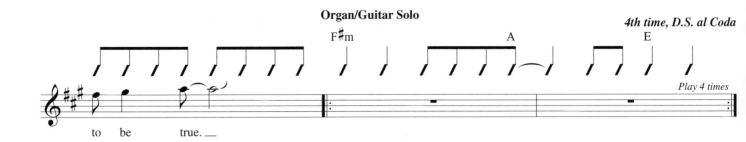

F#m      A      E

*Play 4 times*

to be true. __

**Coda**

*cont. rhy. sim.*

F#m      A      E      F#m      A

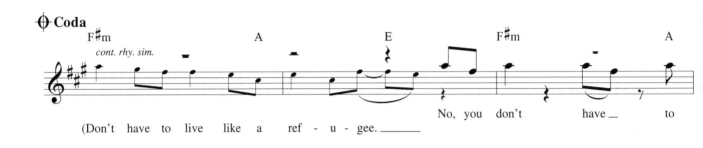

(Don't have to live like a ref - u - gee. _____    No, you don't have __ to

E      F#m      A      E

live like a ref - u - gee. _____    Don't have to live like a ref - u - gee. _____    Ba - by, you

F#m      A      E      F#m      A

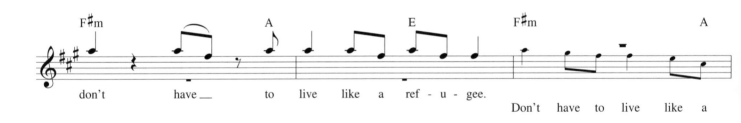

don't have __ to live like a ref - u - gee.    Don't have to live like a

**Outro-Guitar Solo**

*Repeat and fade*

E      F#m      A      E

Oh,    oh,    oh.
ref - u - gee.) _____

*Additional Lyrics*

2. Somewhere, somehow, somebody must have
   Kicked you around some.
   Tell me why you wanna lay there,
   Revel in your abandon.

*Pre-Chorus* 2. Honey, it don't make no diff'rence to me.
   Baby, ev'rybody's had to fight to be free.

3. Somewhere, somehow, somebody must have
   Kicked you around some.
   Who knows? Maybe you were kidnapped,
   Tied up, taken away and held for ransom.

*Pre-Chorus* 3. Honey, it don't really matter to me.
   Baby, ev'rybody's had to fight to be free.

# Runnin' Down a Dream

**Words and Music by Tom Petty, Jeff Lynne and Mike Campbell**

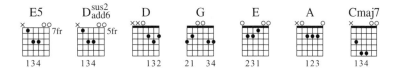

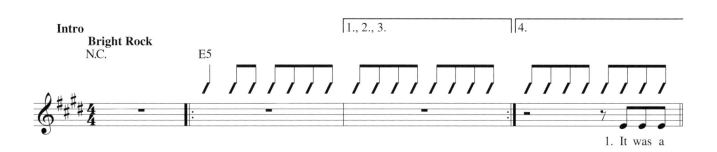

**Intro**
**Bright Rock**
N.C.

1., 2., 3. | 4.

E5

1. It was a

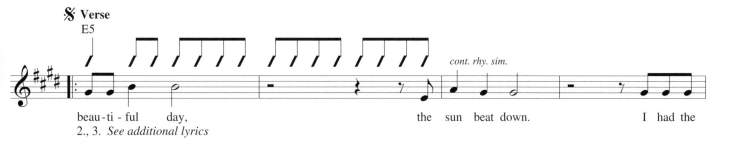

**Verse**
E5

*cont. rhy. sim.*

beau-ti-ful day,     the sun beat down.     I had the
2., 3. *See additional lyrics*

D$^{sus2}_{add6}$     E5

ra-di-o on.     I was driv-in'.     The trees went by,

D$^{sus2}_{add6}$

me and Del were sing-in' _____ lit-tle "Run-a-way."     I was fly-

**Chorus**
E5          D     G     E

-in'.
         Yeah,
         Yeah,  } run-nin' down a dream _____ that
         I'm

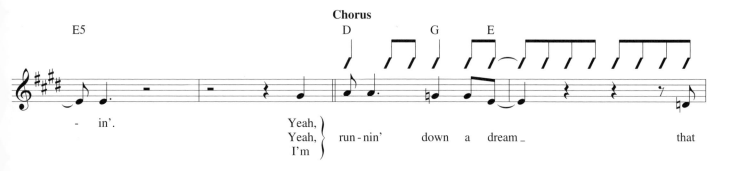

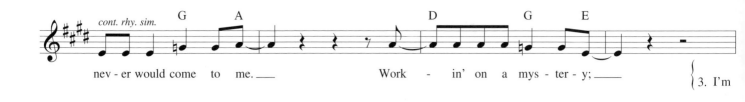

nev - er would come to me. ___ Work - in' on a mys - ter - y; ___

{ 3. I'm

*To Coda* ⊕

1., 2. go - in' wher - ev - er it leads. ___ }
go - in' wher - ev - er it leads. ___ }

Run - nin' down a dream. ___

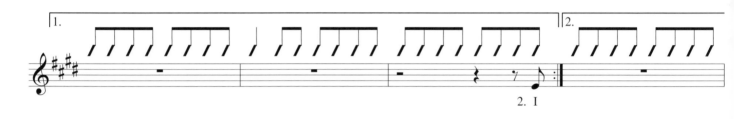

2. I

**Interlude**
Cmaj7

(Woo. ___

D$^{sus2}_{add6}$

*cont. rhy. sim.*

E5

Woo. ___

Woo. ___

*D.S. al Coda*

Cmaj7

D$^{sus2}_{add6}$

Woo. ___

Woo.) ___

⊕ **Coda**

Yeah, I'm

**Chorus**

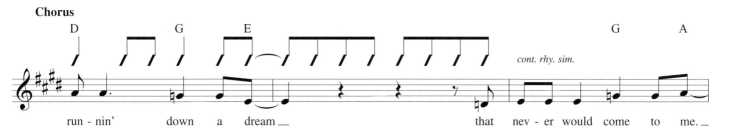

run - nin' down a dream ___ that nev - er would come to me. ___

___ Work - in' on a mys - ter - y; ___ I'm

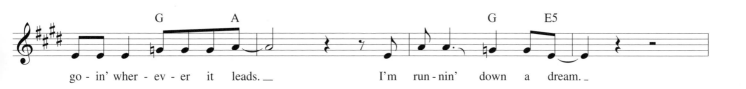

go - in' wher - ev - er it leads. ___ I'm run - nin' down a dream. _

**Outro**

**Repeat and fade**

*Additional Lyrics*

2. I felt so good, like anything was possible.
   Hit cruise control, and rubbed my eyes.
   The last three days, and the rain was unstoppable,
   It was always cold, no sunshine.

3. I rolled on, the sky grew dark.
   I put the pedal down to make some time.
   There's somethin' good waitin' down this road.
   I'm pickin' up whatever's mine.

# Stop Draggin' My Heart Around

**Words and Music by Tom Petty and Mike Campbell**

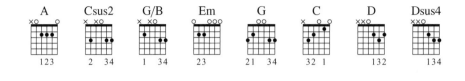

*Stevie Nicks:* 1. Ba - by,

**Verse**

you'll come knock-ing on my __ front door. Same old line you use to

use be - fore. I said, "Ya, __ well, __ what am I sup-posed to do?"

**Pre-Chorus**

I did - n't know what I was get - ting in - to. So you've had a lit - tle

trou - ble in town. __ Now you're keep-ing some de - mon down. ____

**Chorus**

C                                                          D                                          Csus2   G/B        Csus2

Stop   drag-gin' my,          stop   drag-gin' my,          stop   drag-gin' my   heart  a - round.

**Interlude**

Em                                                    G            A          Em                                    G            A

(Oo.) _____

**Verse**

Em                                                    G            A          Em

*cont. rhy. sim.*

*S. Nicks:* 2. It's  hard   to  think  a - bout          what you've   want - ed.            It's  hard  to  think  a - bout
3. *See additional lyrics*

G            A          Em                                              G            A

what   you've   lost.          This   does - n't   have   to   be   the   big   get   e - ven.

Em                                    G            A          Em

This  does - n't   have   to   be ___  an - y - thing   at   all.        *T. Petty:* I   know  you  real - ly   want  to

G            A          Em                                              G            A

tell   me   good - bye.          I   know  you  real - ly  want  to   be   your  own   girl.

**Pre-Chorus**

C                                                          D                                          C

Ba - by,  you  could  nev - er   look   me   in   the   eye. ___          Yeah, you  buck - le   with  the

*Additional Lyrics*

3. There's people running 'round loose in the world,
   Ain't got nothing better to do.
   Than make a meal of some bright-eyed kid,
   You need someone looking after you.
   I know you really want to tell me goodbye.
   I know you really want to be your own girl.

## · AUTHENTIC CHORDS · ORIGINAL KEYS · COMPLETE SONGS ·

The *Strum It* series lets players strum the chords and sing along with their favorite hits. Each song has been select-ed because it can be played with regular open chords, barre chords, or other moveable chord types. Guitarists can simply play the rhythm, or play and sing along through the entire song. All songs are shown in their original keys complete with chords, strum patterns, melody and lyrics. Wherever possible, the chord voicings from the recorded versions are notated.

### Acoustic Classics          00699238 / $10.95
1 classics: And I Love Her • Barely Breathing • Free Fallin' • Maggie May • Mr. Jones • Only Wanna Be with You • Patience • Wonderful Tonight • Yesterday • more.

### The Beach Boys' Greatest Hits          00699357/ $12.95
9 tunes: Barbara Ann • California Girls • Fun, Fun Fun • Good Vibrations • Help Me Rhonda • I Get Around • Surfer Girl • Surfin' U.S.A. • Wouldn't It Be Nice • more.

### The Beatles Favorites          00699249 / $14.95
3 Beatles hits: Can't Buy Me Love • Eight Days a Week • Hey Jude • Let It Be • She Loves You • Yesterday • You've Got to Hide Your Love Away • and more.

### Best of Contemporary Christian          00699531 / $12.95
0 CCM favorites: Awesome God • Butterfly Kisses • El Shaddai • Father's Eyes • I Could Sing of Your Love Forever • Jesus Freak • The Potter's Hand • and more.

### Best of Steven Curtis Chapman          00699530 / $12.95
6 top hits: For the Sake of the Call • Heaven in the Real World • His Strength Is Perfect • I Will Be Here • More To This Life • Signs of Life • What Kind of Joy • more.

### Very Best of Johnny Cash          00699514 / $9.95
7 songs: A Boy Named Sue • Daddy Sang Bass • Folsom Prison Blues • I Walk the Line • The Man in Black • Orange Blossom Special • Ring of Fire • and more.

### Celtic Guitar Songbook          00699265 / $9.95
5 songs: Cockles and Mussels • Danny Boy • The Irish Washerwoman • Kerry Dance • Killarney • My Wild Irish Rose • Sailor's Hornpipe • and more.

### Christmas Songs for Guitar          00699247 / $9.95
0 favorites: Frosty the Snow Man • Grandma Got Run Over by a Reindeer • I'll Be Home for Christmas • Rockin' Around the Christmas Tree • Silver Bells • more.

### Christmas Songs with 3 Chords          00699487 / $8.95
0 all-time favorites: Angels We Have Heard on High • Away in a Manger • Here We Come A-Wassailing • Jolly Old St. Nicholas • Silent Night • Up on the Housetop • more.

### Very Best of Eric Clapton          00699560 / $12.95
0 songs: Change the World • For Your Love • I Shot the Sheriff • Layla • My Father's Eyes • Tears in Heaven • White Room • Wonderful Tonight • and more.

### Country Strummin'          00699119 / $8.95
atures 24 songs: Achy Breaky Heart • Blue • A Broken Wing • Gone Country • I Fall to Pieces • She and I • Unchained Melody • What a Crying Shame • and more.

### Jim Croce – Classic Hits          00699269 / $10.95
2 great songs: Bad, Bad Leroy Brown • I'll Have to Say I Love You in a Song • Operator (That's Not the Way It Feels) • Time in a Bottle • and more.

### Very Best of John Denver          00699488 / $12.95
0 top hits: Leaving on a Jet Plane • Rocky Mountain High • Sunshine on My Shoulders • Take Me Home, Country Roads • Thank God I'm a Country Boy • more.

### Neil Diamond          00699593 / $12.95
6 classics: America • Cracklin' Rosie • Forever in Blue Jeans • Hello Again • I'm a Believer • Love on the Rocks • Song Sung Blue • Sweet Caroline • and more.

### Disney Favorites          00699171 / $10.95
34 Disney favorites: Can You Feel the Love Tonight • Cruella De Vil • Friend Like Me • It's a Small World • Under the Sea • Whistle While You Work • and more.

### Disney Greats          00699172 / $10.95
39 classics: Beauty and the Beast • Colors of the Wind • Go the Distance • Heigh-Ho • Kiss the Girl • When You Wish Upon a Star • Zip-A-Dee-Doo-Dah • and more.

### Best of The Doors          00699177 / $10.95
25 Doors favorites: Been Down So Long • Hello I Love You Won't You Tell Me Your Name? • Light My Fire • Riders on the Storm • Touch Me • and more.

### Favorite Songs with 3 Chords          00699112 / $8.95
27 popular songs: All Shook Up • Boot Scootin' Boogie • Great Balls of Fire • Lay Down Sally • Semi-Charmed Life • Twist and Shout • Wooly Bully • and more.

### Favorite Songs with 4 Chords          00699270 / $8.95
22 tunes: Beast of Burden • Don't Be Cruel • Gloria • I Fought the Law • La Bamba • Last Kiss • Let Her Cry • Love Stinks • Peggy Sue • 3 AM • Wild Thing • and more.

### Fireside Sing-Along          00699273 / $8.95
25 songs: Edelweiss • Leaving on a Jet Plane • Take Me Home, Country Roads • Teach Your Children • This Land Is Your Land • You've Got a Friend • and more.

### Folk Favorites          00699517 / $8.95
42 traditional favorites: Camptown Races • Clementine • Danny Boy • My Old Kentucky Home • Rock-A-My Soul • Scarborough Fair • and more.

### Irving Berlin's God Bless America®          00699508 / $9.95
25 patriotic anthems: America, the Beautiful • Battle Hymn of the Republic • God Bless America • The Star Spangled Banner • This Land Is Your Land • and more.

### Great '50s Rock          00699187 / $9.95
28 hits: At the Hop • Blueberry Hill • Bye Bye Love • Hound Dog • Rock Around the Clock • That'll Be the Day • and more.

### Great '60s Rock          00699188 / $9.95
27 classic rock songs: And I Love Her • Gloria • Mellow Yellow • Return to Sender • Runaway • Surfin' U.S.A. • The Twist • Under the Boardwalk • Wild Thing • more.

### Great '70s Rock          00699262 / $9.95
21 classic hits: Band on the Run • Lay Down Sally • Let It Be • Love Hurts • Ramblin' Man • Time for Me to Fly • Two Out of Three Ain't Bad • Wild World • and more

### Great '80s Rock          00699263 / $9.95
23 favorites: Centerfold • Free Fallin' • Got My Mind Set on You • Kokomo • Should I Stay or Should I Go • Uptown Girl • What I Like About You • and more.

### Great '90s Rock          00699268 / $9.95
17 contemporary hits: If You Could Only See • Iris • Mr. Jones • Only Wanna Be with You • Tears in Heaven • Torn • The Way • You Were Meant for Me • and more.

### Best of Woody Guthrie          00699496 / $12.95
20 songs: Do Re Mi • The Grand Coulee Dam • Roll On, Columbia • So Long It's Been Good to Know Yuh • This Land Is Your Land • Tom Joad • and more.

### John Hiatt Collection          00699398 / $12.95
17 classics: Angel Eyes • Feels Like Rain • Have a Little Faith in Me • Riding with the King • Thing Called Love (Are You Ready for This Thing Called Love) • and more.

### Hymn Favorites          00699271 / $9.95
Includes: Amazing Grace • Down by the Riverside • Holy, Holy, Holy • Just as I Am • Rock of Ages • What a Friend We Have in Jesus • and more.

### Carole King Collection          00699234 / $12.95
20 songs: I Feel the Earth Move • It's Too Late • A Natural Woman • So Far Away • Tapestry • Will You Love Me Tomorrow • You've Got a Friend • and more.

### Very Best of Dave Matthews Band          00699520 / $12.95
12 favorites: Ants Marching • Crash into Me • Crush • Don't Drink the Water • Everyday • The Space Between • Stay (Wasting Time) • What Would You Say • and more.

### Sarah McLachlan          00699231 / $10.95
20 of Sarah's hits: Angel • Building a Mystery • I Will Remember You • Ice Cream • Sweet Surrender • more.

### A Merry Christmas Songbook          00699211 / $8.95
51 holiday hits: Away in a Manger • Deck the Hall • Fum, Fum, Fum • The Holly and the Ivy • Jolly Old St. Nicholas • O Christmas Tree • and more!

### More Favorite Songs with 3 Chords          00699532 / $8.95
27 great hits: Barbara Ann • Gloria • Hang on Sloopy • Hound Dog • La Bamba • Mony, Mony • Rock Around the Clock • Rock This Town • Rockin' Robin • and more.

### Pop-Rock Guitar Favorites          00699088 / $8.95
31 songs: Angie • Brown Eyed Girl • Eight Days a Week • Free Bird • Gloria • Hey Jude • Let It Be • Maggie May • Wild Thing • Wonderful Tonight • and more.

### Elvis! Greatest Hits          00699276 / $10.95
24 Elvis classics: All Shook Up • Always on My Mind • Can't Help Falling in Love • Hound Dog • It's Now or Never • Jailhouse Rock • Love Me Tender • and more.

### Songs for Kids          00699616 / $9.95
28 fun favorites: Alphabet Song • Bingo • Frere Jacques • Kum Ba Yah • London Bridge • Old MacDonald • Pop Goes the Weasel • Yankee Doodle • more.

### Best of George Strait          00699235 / $10.95
20 Strait hits: Adalida • All My Ex's Live in Texas • Carried Away • Does Fort Worth Ever Cross Your Mind • Right or Wrong • Write This Down • and more.

### 25 Country Standards          00699523 / $12.95
Includes: Always on My Mind • Amazed • Elvira • Friends in Low Places • Hey, Good Lookin' • Sixteen Tons • You Are My Sunshine • Your Cheatin' Heart • and more.

### Best of Hank Williams Jr.          00699224 / $10.95
24 signature standards: All My Rowdy Friends Are Coming Over Tonight • Honky Tonkin' • There's a Tear in My Beer • Whiskey Bent and Hell Bound • and more.

### Women of Rock          00699183 / $9.95
22 hits: Don't Speak • Give Me One Reason • I Don't Want to Wait • Insensitive • Lovefool • Stay • Torn • You Oughta Know • You Were Meant for Me • and more.

FOR MORE INFORMATION, SEE YOUR LOCAL MUSIC DEALER, OR WRITE TO:

HAL•LEONARD® CORPORATION
7777 W. BLUEMOUND RD. P.O. BOX 13819 MILWAUKEE, WI 53213

Visit Hal Leonard online at

Prices, contents & availability subject to change without notice.

0604

**VOL. 1 – ROCK GUITAR**     00699570 / $14.95
Day Tripper • Message in a Bottle • Refugee • Shattered • Sunshine of Your Love • Takin' Care of Business • Tush • Walk This Way.

**VOL. 2 – ACOUSTIC**     00699569 / $14.95
Angie • Behind Blue Eyes • Best of My Love • Blackbird • Dust in the Wind • Layla • Night Moves • Yesterday.

**VOL. 3 – HARD ROCK**     00699573 / $14.95
Crazy Train • Iron Man • Living After Midnight • Rock You like a Hurricane • Round and Round • Smoke on the Water • Sweet Child O' Mine • You Really Got Me.

**VOL. 4 – POP/ROCK**     00699571 / $14.95
Breakdown • Crazy Little Thing Called Love • Hit Me with Your Best Shot • I Want You to Want Me • Lights • R.O.C.K. in the U.S.A. • Summer of '69 • What I Like About You.

**VOL. 5 – MODERN ROCK**     00699574 / $14.95
Aerials • Alive • Bother • Chop Suey! • Control • Last Resort • Take a Look Around (Theme from *M:I-2*) • Wish You Were Here.

**VOL. 6 – '90S ROCK**     00699572 / $14.95
Are You Gonna Go My Way • Come Out and Play • I'll Stick Around • Know Your Enemy • Man in the Box • Outshined • Smells Like Teen Spirit • Under the Bridge.

**VOL. 7 – BLUES GUITAR**     00699575 / $14.95
All Your Love (I Miss Loving) • Born Under a Bad Sign • Hide Away • I'm Tore Down • I'm Your Hoochie Coochie Man • Pride and Joy • Sweet Home Chicago • The Thrill Is Gone.

**VOL. 8 – ROCK**     00699585 / $14.95
All Right Now • Black Magic Woman • Get Back • Hey Joe • Layla • Love Me Two Times • Won't Get Fooled Again • You Really Got Me.

**VOL. 9 – PUNK ROCK**     00699576 / $14.95
All the Small Things • Fat Lip • Flavor of the Weak • I Feel So • Lifestyles of the Rich and Famous • Say It Ain't So • Self Esteem • (So) Tired of Waiting for You.

**VOL. 10 – ACOUSTIC**     00699586 / $14.95
Here Comes the Sun • Landslide • The Magic Bus • Norwegian Wood (This Bird Has Flown) • Pink Houses • Space Oddity • Tangled Up in Blue • Tears in Heaven.

**VOL. 11 – EARLY ROCK**     00699579 / $14.95
Fun, Fun, Fun • Hound Dog • Louie, Louie • No Particular Place to Go • Oh, Pretty Woman • Rock Around the Clock • Under the Boardwalk • Wild Thing.

**VOL. 12 – POP/ROCK**     00699587 / $14.95
867-5309/Jenny • Every Breath You Take • Money for Nothing • Rebel, Rebel • Run to You • Ticket to Ride • Wonderful Tonight • You Give Love a Bad Name.

**VOL. 13 – FOLK ROCK**     00699581 / $14.95
Annie's Song • Leaving on a Jet Plane • Suite: Judy Blue Eyes • This Land Is Your Land • Time in a Bottle • Turn! Turn! Turn! • You've Got a Friend • You've Got to Hide Your Love Away.

**VOL. 14 – BLUES ROCK**     00699582 / $14.95
Blue on Black • Crossfire • Cross Road Blues (Crossroads) • The House Is Rockin' • La Grange • Move It on Over • Roadhouse Blues • Statesboro Blues.

**VOL. 15 – R&B**     00699583 / $14.95
Ain't Too Proud to Beg • Brick House • Get Ready • I Can't Help Myself • I Got You (I Feel Good) • I Heard It Through the Grapevine • My Girl • Shining Star.

**VOL. 16 – JAZZ**     00699584 / $14.95
All Blues • Bluesette • Footprints • How Insensitive • Misty • Satin Doll • Stella by Starlight • Tenor Madness.

**VOL. 17 – COUNTRY**     00699588 / $14.95
Amie • Boot Scootin' Boogie • Chattahoochee • Folsom Prison Blues • Friends in Low Places • Forever and Ever, Amen • T-R-O-U-B-L-E • Workin' Man Blues.

**VOL. 18 – ACOUSTIC ROCK**     00699577 / $14.95
About a Girl • Breaking the Girl • Drive • Iris • More Than Words • Patience • Silent Lucidity • 3 AM.

**VOL. 19 – SOUL**     00699578 / $14.95
Get Up (I Feel Like Being) a Sex Machine • Green Onions • In the Midnight Hour • Knock on Wood • Mustang Sally • Respect • (Sittin' On) The Dock of the Bay • Soul Man.

**VOL. 20 – ROCKABILLY**     00699580 / $14.95
Be-Bop-A-Lula • Blue Suede Shoes • Hello Mary Lou • Little Sister • Mystery Train • Rock This Town • Stray Cat Strut • That'll Be the Day.

**VOL. 21 – YULETIDE**     00699602 / $14.95
Angels We Have Heard on High • Away in a Manger • Deck the Hall • The First Noel • Go, Tell It on the Mountain • Jingle Bells • Joy to the World • O Little Town of Bethlehem.

**VOL. 22 – CHRISTMAS**     00699600 / $14.95
The Christmas Song • Frosty the Snow Man • Happy Xmas • Here Comes Santa Claus • Jingle-Bell Rock • Merry Christmas, Darling • Rudolph the Red-Nosed Reindeer • Silver Bells.

**VOL. 23 – SURF**     00699635 / $14.95
Let's Go Trippin' • Out of Limits • Penetration • Pipeline • Surf City • Surfin' U.S.A. • Walk Don't Run • The Wedge.

**VOL. 24 – ERIC CLAPTON**     00699649 / $14.95
Badge • Bell Bottom Blues • Change the World • Cocaine • Key to the Highway • Lay Down Sally • White Room • Wonderful Tonight.

**VOL. 25 – LENNON & McCARTNEY**     00699642 / $14.95
Back in the U.S.S.R. • Drive My Car • Get Back • A Hard Day's Night • I Feel Fine • Paperback Writer • Revolution • Ticket to Ride.

**VOL. 26 – ELVIS PRESLEY**     00699643 / $14.95
All Shook Up • Blue Suede Shoes • Don't Be Cruel • Heartbreak Hotel • Hound Dog • Jailhouse Rock • Little Sister • Mystery Train.

**VOL. 27 – DAVID LEE ROTH**     00699645 / $14.95
Ain't Talkin' 'Bout Love • Dance the Night Away • Hot for Teacher • Just Like Paradise • A Lil' Ain't Enough • Runnin' with the Devil • Unchained • Yankee Rose.

**VOL. 28 – GREG KOCH**     00699646 / $14.95
Chief's Blues • Death of a Bassman • Dylan the Villain • The Grip • Holy Grail • Spank It • Tonus Diabolicus • Zoiks.

**VOL. 29 – BOB SEGER**     00699647 / $14.95
Against the Wind • Betty Lou's Gettin' Out Tonight • Hollywood Nights • Mainstreet • Night Moves • Old Time Rock & Roll • Rock and Roll Never Forgets • Still the Same.

**VOL. 30 – KISS**     00699644 / $14.95
Cold Gin • Detroit Rock City • Deuce • Firehouse • Heaven's on Fire • Love Gun • Rock and Roll All Nite • Shock Me.

**VOL. 31 – CHRISTMAS HITS**     00699652 / $14.95
Blue Christmas • Do You Hear What I Hear • Happy Holiday • I Saw Mommy Kissing Santa Claus • I'll Be Home for Christmas • Let It Snow! Let It Snow! Let It Snow! • Little Saint Nick • Snowfall.

**VOL. 32 – THE OFFSPRING**     00699653 / $14.95
Bad Habit • Come Out and Play • Gone Away • Gotta Get Away • Hit That • The Kids Aren't Alright • Pretty Fly (For a White Guy) • Self Esteem.

**VOL. 33 – ACOUSTIC CLASSICS**     00699656 / $14.95
Across the Universe • Babe, I'm Gonna Leave You • Crazy on You • Heart of Gold • Hotel California • I'd Love to Change the World • Thick As a Brick • Wanted Dead or Alive.

**VOL. 34 – CLASSIC ROCK**     00699658 / $14.95
Aqualung • Born to Be Wild • The Boys Are Back in Town • Brown Eyed Girl • Reeling in the Years • Rock'n Me • Rocky Mountain Way • Sweet Emotion.

**VOL. 35 – HAIR METAL**     00699660 / $14.95
Decadence Dance • Don't Treat Me Bad • Down Boys • Seventeen • Shake Me • Up All Night • Wait • Talk Dirty to Me.

**VOL. 36 – SOUTHERN ROCK**     00699661 / $1
Can't You See • Flirtin' with Disaster • Hold on Loosely • Jessi Mississippi Queen • Ramblin' Man • Sweet Home Alabam What's Your Name.

**VOL. 37 – ACOUSTIC METAL**     00699662 / $1
Every Rose Has Its Thorn • Fly to the Angels • Hole Hearted • Is on the Way • Love of a Lifetime • Signs • To Be with You • W the Children Cry.

**VOL. 38 – BLUES**     00699663 / $1
Boom Boom • Cold Shot • Crosscut Saw • Everyday I Have the B • Frosty • Further On up the Road • Killing Floor • Texas Flood

**VOL. 39 – '80S METAL**     00699664 / $1
Bark at the Moon • Big City Nights • Breaking the Chains • Cu Personality • Lay It Down • Living on a Prayer • Panama • Smo in the Boys Room.

**VOL. 40 – INCUBUS**     00699668 / $1
Are You In? • Drive • Megalomaniac • Nice to Know You • Pa Me • Stellar • Talk Shows on Mute • Wish You Were Here.

**VOL. 41 – ERIC CLAPTON**     00699669 / $1
After Midnight • Can't Find My Way Home • Forever Man • I the Sheriff • I'm Tore Down • Pretending • Running on Fai Tears in Heaven.

**VOL. 42 – CHART HITS**     00699670 / $1
Are You Gonna Be My Girl • Heaven • Here Without You • I Be in a Thing Called Love • Just Like You • Last Train Home • Love • Until the Day I Die.

**VOL. 43 – LYNYRD SKYNYRD**     00699681 / $1
Don't Ask Me No Questions • Free Bird • Gimme Three Ste I Know a Little • Saturday Night Special • Sweet Home Alabar That Smell • You Got That Right.

**VOL. 44 – JAZZ**     00699689 / $1
I Remember You • I'll Remember April • Impressions • Mellow Tone • Moonlight in Vermont • On a Slow Boat to Chi Things Ain't What They Used to Be • Yesterdays.

**VOL. 46 – MAINSTREAM ROCK**     00699722 / $1
Just a Girl • Keep Away • Kryptonite • Lightning Crashes • 19 One Step Closer • Scar Tissue • Torn.

**VOL. 47 – HENDRIX SMASH HITS**     00699723/ $1
All Along the Watchtower • Can You See Me? • Crosstown Tra Fire • Foxey Lady • Hey Joe • Manic Depression • Purple Ha Red House • Remember • Stone Free • The Wind Cries Mary

**VOL. 48 – AEROSMITH CLASSICS**     00699724 / $1
Back in the Saddle • Draw the Line • Dream On • Last Child • M Kin • Same Old Song & Dance • Sweet Emotion • Walk This W

**VOL. 50 – NÜ METAL**     00699726 / $1
Duality • Here to Stay • In the End • Judith • Nookie • So C Toxicity • Whatever.

**VOL. 51 – ALTERNATIVE '90S**     00699727 / $1
Alive • Cherub Rock • Come As You Are • Give It Away • Jane • No Excuses • No Rain • Santeria.

**VOL. 56 – FOO FIGHTERS**     00699749 / $1
All My Life • Best of You • DOA • I'll Stick Around • Learn • Monkey Wrench • My Hero • This Is a Call.

**VOL. 57 – SYSTEM OF A DOWN**     00699751 / $1
Aerials • B.Y.O.B. • Chop Suey! • Innervision • Questio Spiders • Sugar • Toxicity.